Growing and Showing
Fuchsias

Leo B. Boullemier

David & Charles
Newton Abbot   London   North Pomfret (Vt)

By the same author

*Check list of Species Hybrids and Cultivars of the Genus Fuchsia
Fascinating Fuchsias*

British Library Cataloguing in Publication Data

Boullemier, Leo B.
  Growing and showing fuchsias. – (Growing
  and showing)
  1. Fuchsia
  I. Title
  635.9'3344   SB413.F8

  ISBN 0–7153–8592–5

Text and line illustrations © Leo B. Boullemier 1985

Photoset in Souvenir by
Northern Phototypesetting Co, Bolton
Printed in Great Britain by
Redwood Burn Limited, Trowbridge, Wilts
for David & Charles (Publishers) Limited
Brunel House Newton Abbot Devon

Published in the United States of America
by David & Charles Inc
North Pomfret Vermont 05053 USA

Contents

1 Growing For Showing

Growing fuchsias for exhibition offers a challenge and requires dedication. But it is neither difficult nor mysterious. The plants are grown exactly as if for your garden or home, except that they are grown more carefully, with strict attention to detail – the ultimate aim being the production of perfect specimen plants exactly as specified by the show schedule for the classes you choose to enter. It is this attention to detail that brings you exhibition-standard plants as opposed to ordinary ones.

Shows give all of us the chance to see expertly grown plants, so that subsequently we raise our own standards. It is at shows that new cultivars can be seen. To enjoy showing, you need to enter for what you can contribute, rather than for anything you might receive, and if all the aspects of cultivation described through this book are absorbed and practised, you should be able to achieve satisfaction and some success on the showbench.

The Fuchsias we grow

The fuchsia is subtropical in origin. Many fuchsias make vigorous shrubs and trees in their native habitats, usually of heavy rainfall and at high altitude. So their main requirements throughout their growing life are moderate warmth, moisture, shade, humidity and ventilation. In Britain we grow them as either half-hardy or hardy deciduous shrubs, within the following categories:

Species: There are probably around 100 of these. Those seen on the showbenches include *F. arborescens, F. boliviana (F. corymbiflora), F. denticulata, F. fulgens, F. procumbens* and *F. splendens.*

Variants and Varieties: Groups of individuals distinguishable within a species, but not considered a distinct species themselves; or any variation within a species. The term 'variety' should really be kept for variations of the species in wild form, such as *F. magellanica molinae*, which should correctly be named *F. magellanica* variety *molinae*. The International Code of Nomenclature for Cultivated Plants (1961) does, however, use the

Parts of the fuchsia flower

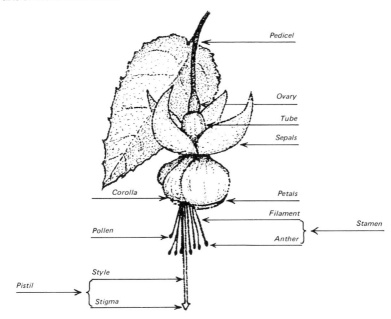

terms 'cultivar' and 'variety' as exact equivalents.

Hybrids: Plants resulting from a cross between parents genetically unlike; the offspring from crossing two different species or their variants.

Cultivars: These, the results of crossing species with hybrids, or hybrids with hybrids, constitute the vast majority of the fuchsias available from hybridists and nurserymen – the horticultural equivalent of the botanical 'variety'.

We have to grow fuchsias somewhat artificially, and with considerable effort to train them to specific shapes, or they would become unmanageable. For show, as this book describes, we repot them regularly, spray the leaves with water on every suitable occasion, take every step to obtain big, clean plants with glossy turgid leaves, free of pests, and with large flowers typical of the variety concerned.

Showbench specimens can be obtained from one season's growth, provided the gradual potting-on process is followed, and that fast, vigorous cultivars are selected; examples are Border Queen, Bon Accorde, Lady Isobel Barnett, Mieke Meursing, Rufus. They will finalise in a 5in (12.5cm) or even 6in (15cm) pot. The majority of plants for the showbench are, however, two- or three-year-old plants, or have been grown on the biennial method, described in Chapter 4.

2 Cultivation and Winter Care

Growers will know how to take cuttings of their fuchsias, and for the would-be exhibitor success depends on the type of cutting selected rather than the method used. Always choose a cutting without bud or flower: if there is one, remove it – the plant needs all its energy for root formation. Look for cuttings with three leaves instead of the usual two at each axil. Checkerboard, Snowcap and Mephisto are typical of varieties that offer these.

Cuttings should be as soft as possible, and taken as early in the New Year as possible. I strongly recommend the small tip-cutting: just the tip, consisting of either one or two pairs of leaves and the growing-tip. This produces a much stronger plant, with roots and shoots at and below soil level. This is most desirable for exhibition plants, especially those to be trained as bushes or shrubs for 3½in (9cm) pot work.

Immerse cuttings in water before striking, and insert them a little deeper into the striking medium than you usually do at potting-on and potting-off stages. For striking, a mixture of 80 per cent Humber or good soilless compost with 20 per cent Perlite is good. When potting-off rooted cuttings, do not over-pot; a 2in (5cm) or at most 2½in (6.25cm) pot produces larger root growth which in turn produces larger top growth.

Soils and Composts

The soil or compost for exhibition plants is most important. My own first choice is John Innes No 2, if *good* John Innes is available; and if for exhibition purposes, I put it in clay pots. But inferior composts are sold today, with the main ingredient, loam, replaced by almost any material. The John Innes Manufacturers' Association, Horticultural Trades Association, Reading, Berkshire, may be able to help you find a reliable supplier. If you have difficulty, use a proprietary soilless compost. These give excellent results. (For myself, I have been pleased with Humber Soilless Compost, from Humber Manures Ltd, Stoneferry, Hull.)

(*above*) Fine batch of autumn-struck cuttings in polystyrene trays, ready for first potting in early February; (*below left*) First potting of an autumn-struck cutting. Note the finger pressure only, with thumbs outside the pot; (*below right*) Root system ready for potting into third pot. (Tap pot sharply on bench, holding plant as shown.) Note the fine root system obtained with Humber soilless compost

If you wish to mix your own compost, my own soil-based formula (it assumes you can get good loam and do not object to using it unsterilised) is: 2 parts loam, 1 part sphagnum peat, 1 part coarse (3–4mm) sand or grit. To this is added 4oz (113g) of John Innes base fertiliser to each bushel, but for fuchsias not the chalk that is present in the JI commercial formula. (They tolerate chalk, but it does not particularly benefit them.)

So use either soilless or soil-based compost for your fuchsias, but never mix the two, or drastically alter the ingredients or the formulas. Use clay pots for loam-based composts, plastic pots for soilless. Any mixing of these combinations will not produce showbench plants.

Feeding

Fuchsias are heavy feeders, particularly when established; without a balanced diet the blooms are fewer, smaller and of poorer colour. When they are grown in pots the resources of the soil must be supplemented. Give a weak feed as soon as young plants are established in their first 2in (5cm) pots, and continue feeding throughout the plant's life except in winter. Use fertilisers with a high nitrogen content in the early stages of growth; switch to a high-potash fertiliser as plants bud or come into flower. Standardise on a certain strength of your selected fertiliser, giving more if needed by making more frequent applications, not by increasing the strength.

Never feed plants that are dry at the roots; if necessary water thoroughly an hour or so before feeding. And never feed a sickly-looking plant. Even fuchsias can be over-fed, producing too much lush growth, especially when you are concentrating on giving nitrogen. If also over-potted they then become huge plants without flower and prone to disease. Never give fertiliser at more than the strength indicated on the label.

Whether organic or inorganic, fertilisers contain nitrogen, phosphorus (phosphates) and potassium (potash), referred to as N–P–K. Nitrogen (N) stimulates the growth of leaves, gives dark green foliage, and increases the size of the plant. Phosphates (P_2O_5) stimulate the growth of the root system and speed up flowering. Bonemeal (6 per cent P) is generally applied, being slow-acting and organic. Potash (K_2O) is most essential for fuchsias: without it the plants cannot make full use of the nitrogen for leaf and stem growth, and it helps to prevent soft growth, improves the colour of flowers and increases resistance to disease (see table below).

	NITROGEN	PHOSPHATES	POTASH	
Bio Instant Food	5.2%	5.2%	6%	
Bio Instant No 5	19.1	19.1	22.3	
Bio Instant No 8	36.0	0	12.0	
New Bio	15.0	15.0	20.0	
Boots General	9.3	6.8	4.2	
Boots Tomato	4.0	4.0	7.0	
Growmore	7.0	7.0	7.0	
Humber E	7.0	7.0	7.0	
John Innes Base	5.1	7.2	9.7	
X Liquinure	9.0	6.6	4.1	*Cul.*
Pokon	16.0	21.0	27.0	
Murphy's Double FF	22.0	21.0	17.0	
Maxicrop Tomato	5.1	5.1	6.7	
X Phostrogen	9.7	10.0	26.5	
Sangral General	9.0	5.0	4.0	
Sangral Tomato	6.0	5.0	7.0	
X Tomorite	4.5	6.3	7.0	*Flwr.*
Vitafeed 101	26.0	0	26.0	
Vitafeed 102	18.0	0	36.0	
Vitafeed 103	13.0	0	43.0	
Vitafeed 301	36.0	0	12.0	
Vitax Q4	5.3	6.8	10.0	
Vitax Q4HN	10.0	6.8	10.2	

A Fertiliser Recipe

If you wish to make up your own fertiliser for your exhibition plants, I suggest: 5 parts by weight of sulphate of ammonia; 5 parts by weight of superphosphates; 2 parts by weight of sulphate of potash. This produces an analysis of 8 per cent N, 8 per cent P and 8 per cent K, a nicely balanced fertiliser.

Some growers believe that animal manures are good, but they are in fact low in NPK value.

Trace Elements

Essential for good cultivation – a large reserve is found in good composts. An important one is magnesium. When plants are grown in the same compost for a lengthy time, the supply of magnesium becomes exhausted; the shortage is indicated by yellow streaks and spots on the leaves – the lower leaves eventually drop off. If not corrected, general yellowing of the foliage follows and decay sets in. The remedy is simple enough: a tablespoon of Epsom Salts to a gallon (4.5 litres) of water, applied just two or three times at the earliest indications of trouble.

Another cause of yellowing, this time of the upper leaves, is a deficiency of iron. A remedy is to give sulphate of iron (ferrous sulphate) at the rate of one tablespoon to a gallon of water; give two or three applications.

Foliar Feeding

Plants do absorb some nourishment through their leaves. Whilst recommending spraying once a week with a suitable fertiliser, such as FF or Double F (22 per cent N, 21 per cent P and 17 per cent K), I consider it good only as a tonic feed; and the fertiliser can be used only up to bud stage.

For an immediate boost for backward plants, or to bring along slow specimen plants quickly from bud stage, you can use nitrate of potash (saltpetre). This contains a high ratio of nitrogen ($12\frac{1}{2}$ per cent) and potash (40 per cent), in a form quickly absorbed by the plant. Give one half-teaspoon per pot, watered well in; but use it sparingly. It is expensive, and although putting a lot into the plants it also takes a lot out.

One fertiliser I refer to as a dark secret. It is cheap, although not easy to obtain – soot. This is a straight fertiliser; although it contains only a small proportion of nitrogen, varying from 1 per cent to 7 per cent, it has some sulphur and useful trace elements. Use only soot obtained from the flues of a coal-burning fire, and it must be stored and weathered under cover for at least three months. Light fluffy soot contains more nitrogen than the heavier, dense types. My method is to fill a linen bag holding some 12oz (340g), and immerse it in a two-gallon watering can for at least ten days, then water it down to the colour of weak tea and apply it twice a week, in addition to the normal feeding programme. It imparts a sheen to the foliage and improves the colour of the blooms almost unbelievably.

Stopping

The most important task of preparing fuchsia plants for exhibition is stopping or pinching. To obtain a specimen plant of good shape with maximum growth and flowers, pinch out the strong growths several times. Haphazard stopping produces uneven growth.

The leaves of the fuchsia grow normally in opposite pairs. After stopping, the buds left in the axil of a leaf will produce shoots pointing in the same direction as that leaf. The timing of stopping is important, because if done too early you might remove the small shoots, together with the pair of small leaves. On the other hand, pinching back too late results in checking the growth. Decide, therefore, before pinching, in which direction you wish your new shoots to develop. One method is to observe when new pairs of leaves forming in the axil are pointing in the direction of your line of growth. Not until the shoot is sufficiently large should you remove approximately 6 to 8mm ($\frac{1}{4}$in) of it, making sure you do not damage or remove those tender new buds. The best implement is the thumb and fingernail. Fine-pointed scissors may be necessary for small growth but can crush the fine tissue.

From the resultant growth, according to your choice, one, two or three pairs of leaves are left to develop. With one or three pairs, the plant will branch out at right angles. With two pairs, it will branch in the same direction as the original. It is now assumed that when growth is pinched out, the shoot being stopped already carries the very small green buds which are removed. Approximately 6 weeks later, the shoots that come as the result of this stopping will just be in flower.

Plants can be timed for certain dates. Advice on this in the past has been too loose and not allowed long enough. Six weeks between stopping and flowering for singles, and 8 weeks for doubles, is acceptable only with very early-flowering cultivars and in very favourable conditions. A shoot that has no sign of a bud should not be stopped, unless in the early stages of training. Should you stop this type of shoot, you must add on to the 6-week period the time that would have elapsed to produce buds on the original shoot.

When buds first show on one shoot, it is almost certain that within 7 to 10 days buds will appear on all growing-tips. The strong growing-tips should all be stopped, provided one or two shoots are showing bud at least 8 weeks before your final flowering date.

This period gives time not only for the new growth to make flower, but also the secondary growth. If the first blooms come in 6 weeks, the main flush will follow approximately 2 weeks later. It is considered more correct to allow approximately 60 days for singles, 70 days for semi-doubles and 80 days for doubles, after their final stopping, to reach maximum flowering potential on the showbenches.

Remember that to obtain perfect flowering balance, every time you stop you must make all the stops at the same time.

As it is the main flush we require, do not be afraid to obtain plants with their first flush of flowers, always of superior quality. Provided you feed regularly with a fertiliser with a high potash content at that time, the plants will continue to flower.

Shading

Fuchsias resent high temperatures and excessive variations; an even 65–75°F (18–24°C) would be ideal. During the summer, plants will not grow at a temperature over 75°F (24°C). They are transpiring the water through their leaves to remain alive – another reason most successful showmen give their plants spells of outside conditions once the late spring frosts have finished. This produces good sturdy plants without the need for staking. Some stand the pots in a sheltered position on a bed of gravel, with frequent damping down; others place them on a piece of lawn, where they receive the humidity rising from the grass. An excellent way of preventing plants being blown over by wind is to insert four strong canes, the height of the pot, in the ground around each pot. Return the plants to the greenhouse 2 or 3 weeks before the show to complete their flowering.

Those plants in the greenhouse during the summer months need shading. Lath-type blinds for greenhouses are ideal but expensive; green polythene blinds fitted inside are quite effective, but play havoc with colour renderings. Several types of plastic mesh give excellent results, but never lay the mesh flat on the glass; always leave at least 1in (2.5cm) between it and the glass, or you will increase the heat instead of lowering it. Most of us resort to painting-on a permanent shading; white is the best colour as it reflects back more heat. 'Coolglass' is good and readily obtainable. If you require the cheapest method, mix ordinary plain flour or whitening with water, adding a little salt to aid adhesion. Decorators' size is even better. Apply your shading early: I apply a thin coat of it around Eastertime, and when plants are more mature, in bud and flower, give an extra coat, to prolong their life.

A new type of shading works wonders for me – a non-toxic product called Varishade, developed by Solar Sunstill Inc, USA, but available from most good garden shops and centres. It shades out excessive solar light and heat when dry, and when wet with rain becomes practically transparent; when it dries it becomes opaque again. When it is applied to the inside glass, the normal condensation, which can often linger up to 10am or so, will keep the shading transparent – particularly useful during spring, early summer and autumn. Spray, brush or roller it on; remove by washing when the season is finished.

Watering

Fuchsias are thirsty plants, especially when established in their final pots, and need lots of clean water. Rain or tap? Some growers collect what rainwater they can, but it must be filtered, and I admit I use tap water, even though in my area it is hard.

The old way of testing whether plants needed watering was to tap the pot – clay pots produce a ringing sound if the compost is dry, or a dull, dead one if it is adequately moist. Now that we nearly all use plastic pots and soilless composts, this method is useless. Learn to judge the moisture content by weight: experience will soon tell you whether a pot feels heavy or light; if heavy leave it alone, if light water it well; if in doubt leave it until next time. When watering, really soak the compost. Then leave it alone until just before the plants need watering again; then give another good soaking. The plants' growing potential is at its maximum just before they need water. Never give little dribbles every day.

Always water from the top; provided the drainage is correct, the plant will absorb all the water it requires. If you water from the bottom, the plant could stand with its feet in water for some period, so the soil becomes waterlogged, the roots cannot breathe and in some cases plants die. If you must use saucers, drain away any surplus water still there after a couple of hours or so.

In warm conditions I use the hosepipe for damping down, but never to water the plants. The pressure is too great, and water direct from the mains supply is too cold and likely to check growth.

All plants should be treated individually and watered only when necessary. Always try to finish watering by early afternoon; unless absolutely necessary never water at night. Those who go out to work may have to water in the evening, but it is bad practice, because you are adding to the moisture already present in the night air, which cannot be absorbed. This can cause damping-off of flowers and the premature dropping of buds.

Fuchsias in pots outside will need watering at times, even when it is actually raining; it takes at least four hours of continuous rain to equal the moisture content in a can.

Fuchsias dislike high temperatures, but during very hot spells over-watering is often fatal. In hot weather do not add more water to a pot or basket that already feels moist, even if the plants are limp and wilted. Lightly spray the foliage first and wait to see if the plant picks up. If not, start checking for drainage or over-watering. Do not leave plants in plastic pots in the midday sun.

Winter Care

The two vital overwintering points are that plants must be frost-free and must never be allowed to dry out. This section deals with plants flowered the previous summer, now requiring winter rest, not those grown on the biennial method – discussed in Chapter 5.

As autumn approaches, the ripening of the wood is the first stage of preparing plants for their winter rest. If plants are not already outside, put them out at the end of August, exposing their growth for the maturing and gradual ripening of the wood. Plants will withstand the vigours of the forthcoming winter much better with ripe wood than with young, green, sappy growth. Although at this time you have normally stopped feeding, two or three applications of a high-potash fertiliser, such as sulphate of potash (48.8 per cent K), at the rate of one teaspoon to the gallon (4.5 litres), or Phostrogen (26.5 per cent K), will assist in hardening-off the plants.

In early September discard any plants that did not come up to expectations. Gradually withhold water, encouraging plants to lose their yellowing bottom leaves, but never let them become dust-dry.

Pots laid on their sides close together underneath the staging, ready for a complete covering of moist peat for the winter

Forget about autumn pruning; leave it for the very early spring. You can, however, trim the plants back by removing about one-third of the growth made during the summer. Autumn pruning is not desirable because of the chance of dieback if you cut whilst the sap is high in the stem.

If you have any plants still in the greenhouse, leave all the ventilators wide open, and the doors too when suitable, until the first frost. When the plants are brought back into the greenhouse, aim to keep the temperature at 40°F (4°C), especially for species and triphyllas. Whips, and plants being trained as standards, espaliers and similar shapes, and many autumn-struck cuttings, need to be kept in green leaf, just ticking over, during the winter, together with those plants growing on the biennial method (see page 24).

About the end of October or early November the remaining plants will show signs of requiring their winter rest. If they have not shed their foliage, remove all leaves, leaving just bare stems and framework. Overwinter these plants by keeping them slightly moist in a temperature no higher than 33°F (1°C); they will even stand a degree or two of frost, provided it is not of long duration. Even if you have no artificial heat, it is still possible to overwinter successfully. This time it matters little where you store the plants – the greenhouse, cold frame, garage, shed or even the spare bedroom – provided it is *frost-free*. Without any heat, I store them under the greenhouse staging after giving them a good watering; this is essential for maintaining moisture during the winter. The trimmed plants are laid down in their pots, side by side, standards first, then all the tall trained structures, followed by the bush or shrub types. These are packed together as close as possible, one on top of the other on their sides. The whole lot are then completely covered with sphagnum peat, neither dry nor wet, but just nicely moist. Stems, together with the whole pot, supports and labels, are completely covered, leaving no trace of the plant visible. Apart from a check once or twice during the winter, they are left until the first week in March. They are then unearthed, with young, fresh, pink eyes already showing, in time to be pruned.

This method is almost foolproof, provided you do not get the peat too wet; then mildew and botrytis could be a problem. If the winter is not severe, wherever you store your plants, a covering of sacking, brown paper or even newspaper when frosts are forecast can be adequate, but the winter has to be mild. (Another method, but one that is unlikely to interest the exhibitor, is to commit the plants to Nature by burying them in a trench in the open ground.)

Pruning

The fuchsia is a deciduous shrub and as described above it needs a few months' rest during the winter. After that it is necessary to prune the wood. As rose growers are, the fuchsiaman is faced with two alternatives for pruning: some advocate doing it in the autumn, whereas most experienced growers favour the winter or very early spring. As already mentioned, the disadvantage with autumn pruning is that unless the wood has more or less completely ripened you are pruning green, sappy growth, and dieback will follow.

Firstly, why do we prune? To control the size of the plant; to encourage the formation of new wood; for flowers, remembering that the fuchsia only flowers on new wood; and to encourage new growth.

When do we prune? It all depends upon the conditions prevailing, on how much heat is at your command and on the condition of your plants. Pruning normally takes place during January, February or March, but the real answer is *just before the sap begins to rise.*

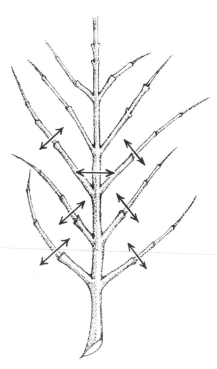

Hard pruning for exhibition, back to one pair of eyes

The end of January or the beginning of February is the ideal time to commence spraying your plants with clear tepid water on every suitable occasion: typical good days are when the sky is blue and the sun shining, with temperatures under glass around 60°F (15.6°C) to 70°F (21.1°C), but perhaps down in the 30°sF outside – making certain that no moisture is present after late afternoon. The spraying operation softens the wood and encourages the formation of the new pink eyes; that helps us by giving an indication of where the new shoots will come, enabling us to shape the plants. As yet the newly awakening plants could not cope with being heavily watered.

And where do we prune? Firstly, cut away all dead and spindly growth, especially misplaced branches and those growing over each other; open out the plant. Then adopt the principle of cutting away approximately two-thirds of last year's growth – or to describe this in another way, prune back to one or two pairs of eyes on each lateral. Having said that, you do have to decide on light, medium or hard pruning. Hard pruning, favoured by most exhibitors, is cutting back to one pair of eyes. Medium pruning is cutting back to two pairs. Light pruning, back to three pairs of eyes, is not to be favoured, as resultant growth will not be strong. Standard fuchsias should be pruned back rather hard in order to obtain more branching near to the head. Baskets, if you use old plants, need hard pruning, to prevent a bare centre. Outside hardies are not pruned until the new growth appears from the base of the plant.

Lastly, remember not to leave pruning until too late in the spring, as you may experience dieback when the sap has risen. Should such cuts have to be made, put a suitable sealing compound on the wounds.

Repotting

As mentioned in the section above on pruning, the old plants are sprayed in the very early spring or late winter to soften the wood, encourage the eyes to form and help the resultant green shoots. When these green shoots appear, or have possibly made a pair of leaves, the important task of repotting takes place. Some successful growers believe that plants that flowered the previous year should be repotted every year. Others repot every two years or not at all. This latter method involves heavy feeding, coupled with hard top and root pruning. It results in short growth, due to restricted root growth. Botanists will tell you that the amount of top growth is controlled by the amount of growth underneath the soil. That is why I prefer the method of repotting each year. The second method produces much smaller leaves and smaller flowers; although these will be more numerous, with the hard pruning, you will get low compact growth which can sometimes be compared with that of a tightly clipped privet hedge, or a plant resembling flowers on a pin-cushion.

Repotting is an important operation and a completely different procedure from potting or potting-on. First, a plant which flowered the previous year should have most of the old soil removed; a strong plant label is useful for this task. Try not to damage any new roots just forming – distinguishable by being white in colour, whereas the old roots are brown. Any damaged roots or excessive root growth can be pruned, but be careful with tap roots, which can bleed when cut.

After this, plant back into a clean pot, slightly larger than the ball of roots and soil left on the plant, using fresh compost. Usually this means repotting into a pot one size smaller; until the plant is again growing vigorously, you do not want too much soil unoccupied by roots. With over-watering, that could result in the soil turning sour. Often you will be repotting from 6in (15cm) to 4in (10cm) pots and from 5in (12.5cm) to 3½in (9cm) pots. You will not produce a plant with showbench potential without this repotting.

When the plant has recovered from the pruning and repotting operations, and has its roots nicely running around the side of the pot, as temperatures are rising in the spring, it can be potted up. Repotting should be carried out as necessary throughout the life of the plant. But once plants of some age are established in the desired-size pot, usually a large one, it may be necessary, after carefully removing the old soil, to move them into a pot of the same size again. If this is not possible, remove any crocks and some of the old soil at the base, and also the top 2in (5cm), and replace with new compost. Large standards and specimen plants in tubs or large pots particularly require this treatment.

The problem of when and when not to water repotted plants can be answered by advising that you restrict water for 24 or even 48 hours, the time when plants start searching with their hair roots for moisture and food. Watering too soon after repotting can restrict this activity. Therefore water with a fine-rosed can after a day or two, having used a compost which is nicely moist but not wet. Further watering may not be needed for another week. Carry on with a light mist spray rather than any heavy watering.

3 Pests and Diseases

Never take plants to shows with pest-bearing foliage or disease. Believe it or not, plants suffering from pests or rust are seen on the showbenches. I would like to see regulations allowing show managers to refuse to admit such plants, as they can in the USA. Any plant affected with either pest or disease will be totally rejected by any recognised judge.

Prevention is essential. Maintain strict hygiene at all times – keep the greenhouse clean, and pathways and ground should be clear of all material, whether rubbish or otherwise. Should you use gravel or sand beds or benches, wash or change them every year. Use Jeyes Fluid at every opportunity when washing down; even the odd watering or spraying with this disinfectant is beneficial. In an empty greenhouse sulphur candles will kill any pests – everything, including yourself if left behind. Always keep an insecticide aerosol handy. Never let any pest or disease get a hold. If you create the correct atmosphere with humidity of 45 to 60 per cent, and keep up scrupulous cleanliness, most troubles will be deterred. Humidity during the late spring and summer must be maintained by constant damping down and spraying. Get a hygrometer (obtainable at a very modest price). As most pests are located on the underside of leaves examine your plants at least once a week.

Spray or fumigate? I prefer fumigating, especially at bud or flower stage, so that there is no risk of marking the blooms, and during the winter so that the creation of a damp atmospheric condition is avoided. Fumigation and spraying should always be carried out in fairly high temperatures, around 65°F (18.4°C), for effective control; do them preferably in the early evening or during dull cloudy weather. When using any sprays add a teaspoon of household detergent to each gallon (4.5 litres), as a wetting agent to assist the spray to sit on the plant. Make sure that the undersides of the leaves are thoroughly wet. Plants should not be dry at the roots when this is done.

Pests

Aphids: These can be found in clusters, green, pink or black; they are the most prolific of all insect pests. Their presence is usually indicated by leaf-curl, caused as they suck the sap from the plant. Their sticky secretion attracts ants and encourages the growth of unsightly sooty moulds, which check the breathing pores of the leaves. Control: HCH, pyrethrum, Murphy's systemic insecticide.

Ants: These can be troublesome by tunnelling and moving soil around, and can spread aphids. They like dry atmospheric conditions. Control: HCH, pyrethrum.

Bees: Although not classified as a pest they can do untold damage, especially in the greenhouse, with their big clumsy feet whilst they search for nectar. They will bruise and mark blooms enough to render them unfit for exhibition. As they are daytime visitors, difficult to control, the only real solution is to cover ventilators and doors with suitable mesh or netting.

Capsid bug: These small green or brown insects ¼in (5.5mm) long, with long legs, similar to greenfly, will disappear under the

Section of the author's greenhouse in early April. Note the cleanliness – and the empty basket stands

leaves at the slightest touch. They puncture the leaves with small holes and suck the sap, causing the leaves to blister and turn red. Shoots often turn blind. This is an outdoor pest, found only occasionally under glass. Control: HCH, Lindane, malathion, nicotine, Tumblebug.

Elephant hawk-moth caterpillar: The young caterpillars, green and brown in colour, are large and destructive; even one, in the greenhouse, will devour the entire leaves of a plant in a night. They may feed on fuchsias, honeysuckle, lilac and petunia, though the true host plant is willow-herb. The effective control is hand picking, especially at night; and for the sake of conservation of a magnificent moth, if possible transfer them gently to wild willow-herb plants.

Fuchsia mite (Aculops fuchsiae): Although not known as yet in Britain, it is spreading in the USA. The mite belongs to the family *Eriophyidae* and damages the growing-points and flowers. Early stages look similar to damage from a heavy aphid infestation or a fungus, with leaf tissues thickened and distorted. Later the leaves or flowers become grotesquely malformed, the leaves resembling those attacked by peach-leaf curl, with increased hairiness and small knob-like leaves at the nodes. The fuchsia mite is almost microscopic (approximately one-seventy-fifth of an inch (0.34mm) in length), yellowish in colour and sucks out plant juices, transferring the substance which deforms the leaves. It looks different from the spider mite, being worm-like with only two pairs of legs. The mites overwinter as eggs or dormant adults in leaf-bud scales, then feed in the spring on the opening buds and new leaves. Chemicals are not yet available in Britain.

Leaf hopper: Green in colour, similar to but smaller than the capsid bug. Causes a coarse white mottling on upper leaf surfaces, and may be found either inside or out. Control: HCH, Lindane, malathion.

Red spider: The worst pest of all for fuchsias. Difficult to detect in early stages, this is really a sucking mite and not a spider. Foliage turns to a bronzy colour, and becomes brittle. Plants badly attacked can be completely defoliated; with a magnifying glass you may even detect the very fine webs. The mites are extremely small, visible as a sort of rust on the underside of leaves. A hot dry atmosphere encourages this pest; moist, humid conditions are inimical to it. When affected, spray or fumigate all your plants every three days until the pest has cleared. Use azobenzene smoke, derris, malathion, Sybol 2 or Murphy's systemic insecticide.

Thrips: Minute insects $\frac{1}{10}$in (2.5mm) long, elongated, with four long narrow wings, dark in colour in adult stage, dirty white when young. They are more often found outside than inside. This is another insect which thrives upon hot, dry conditions and hates the sprayer. Most damage is done in the nymph stage, when the continual sucking of the sap results in silver spotting of foliage which may acquire a pepper-and-salt appearance. Flowers can also be affected. Under glass, if not controlled, thrips may breed continuously. Control: HCH, derris, Lindane, malathion, nicotine, Sybol 2.

Vine weevil: A grub that does untold damage. The grub is $\frac{3}{8}$in (1.5mm) long, crescent-shaped and white with a mahogany-brown head, and it eats away the roots under the soil, in late winter or early spring. The adult beetle, matt black in colour, cuts out irregular pieces from the edges of leaves – you could think it was caterpillar damage. The best control is in late spring or early summer to eradicate the beetle before egg-laying. Effective smokes are Fumite HCH Cones, or Murfume Lindane Smoke Pellets. The best dust is Murphy Gamma HCH Dust. Once you have grubs, control them by watering thoroughly with Gamma HCH, diluted as for normal spraying.

Wasps: Can render flowers useless for show work by eating and chewing away stamens, pistils and even petals, in their search for nectar at the top of the tube. Unlike the bee, who enters the flowers by the correct entrance, wasps usually bore a hole high in the tube in their impatience to obtain nectar. Being daytime visitors, spraying is of little effect. Keeping them out with small-mesh wire or net, as for bees, is the real remedy. If you do have to spray them, use derris, HCH or pyrethrum.

White fly: The tiny fly, about a twenty-fifth of an inch (1mm) long, is covered with white wax. When disturbed, it takes off to another cover, always on the underside of leaves. Another sucker, which deposits honeydew, which in turn produces sooty-mould fungus and closes up the pores of leaves. An attack of white fly can become serious, as it is difficult to eradicate; you kill the adults but you are left with the babies. Use appropriate sprays and smokes at intervals of five days until the pest is cleared: HCH, Lindane, malathion, resmethrin, Sprayday, Picket G or Murphy's systemic insecticide.

Woodlice: Small grey crustaceans $\frac{1}{4}$in (5.5mm) long; may eat both roots and foliage of young plants. Strict hygiene keeps them away. Dust or spray with antkiller, HCH or pyrethrum, or fumigate.

Diseases

Anyone exhibiting fuchsias must be conversant with, and able to control, the two diseases botrytis and rust. Magnificent show plants can be so seriously affected with one of these diseases before showbench date that they become useless.

Botrytis (grey mould): Easily identifiable by the grey, hairy mould. Most prevalent in winter and spring, it affects all types of plants, turning both stems and leaves brown and eventually black. Avoid overcrowding, especially when ventilation is poor. Poor air circulation during the colder months, with high humidity, gives the conditions for botrytis – cold, dank, stale and stagnant; get a good circulation of air, by either ventilation or heat; running an electric fan just to get the air circulating is worthwhile. As a remedy, use a fungicide such as benomyl or captan. Benlate is extremely effective, but use the new Benlate by ICI to which Activex has been added – they claim it leaves foliage with a natural glossy finish. Other sprays include captan, Strike, thiram, Hexyl, or if a fumigant is desired, tecnazene – Murphy's Pest and Disease Smoke.

During the growing period, too, particularly the short period before exhibition, make sure no plant overlaps another – not by one leaf.

Rust: This has always been a problem with fuchsias, and it can even be 'brought in' from some specialist nurserymen. Readily identified by the reddish-brown and orange spore-patches or pustules on the underside of the leaves, showing as yellow or black spots on the upper surface. Rust can be carried on the wind, most likely from its wild host plant, the willow-herb, or by bees. Outbreaks of rust are usually found first inside the greenhouse door, or near open roof-lights; the spread then depends upon the direction of draughts. It prevents light from getting to the leaves, restricts the amount of food produced and so stunts growth; and it is extremely contagious. The sure cure is picking off all affected leaves by hand and burning them, and maintaining that buoyant atmosphere with good air circulation.

Effective controls are the relatively new products Nimrod T from ICI and Plantvax 75 by Uniroyal, but the latter is not generally available yet to the amateur grower. Nimrod T is formulated as a liquid for systemic control and contains bupirimate and triforine; it is a great improvement on the general garden fungicides containing thiram.

4 Training – and Biennial Cultivation

Shows at both national and local level include classes for many types of plants, trained to specific shapes, with the bush or shrub shape being predominant. Fashions change in every aspect of life, however, and in fuchsia cultivation and training there have been innovations in recent years: the miniature standard, the hanging pot and growing on the biennial method.

Biennial Cultivation

There are many methods of growing fuchsias. Three are commonly known as current growth cultivation, normal growth cultivation, with pruning and repotting in the late winter or early spring, and – the more advanced method – biennial cultivation. This latter is far superior, and is the method by which most top exhibitors in this country obtain their huge show specimens, especially those trained as shrub plants.

Biennial plants are those which are not allowed to flower until their second year. Start by taking a cutting in the early months of the summer, May or June. Then you will find choice material available, either from stock plants or young plants. Take it as soft and green as possible; if three-leaved shoots are available, these are the best. When rooted, normally after 14 to 18 days, pot the cuttings off singly into either 2in (5cm) or 2¼in (5.5cm) pots. Use good soilless compost if using plastic pots.

No heat is necessary at this time of year. Cultivate as usual, potting-on lin (2.5cm) at a time, stopping and feeding. Grow the young plants as hard as possible by standing them out in the open during the summer, or in a cold frame. The objective is to establish a strong, sturdy framework to work upon the following year – this first year the plant is not to be allowed to flower. This is achieved and controlled by regular stopping and pinching-out.

By September or October the plant is growing in a 4in (10cm) or a 5in (12.5cm) pot, the latter size being the maximum; you are now encouraging the plant to go into a semi-dormant state, by means of gradually withholding water and feed. During the months of November to January the plant must just 'tick over'.

Here comes the first disadvantage: the temperature needed is 40°F (4.4°C) minimum and a maximum of 45°F (7.2°C), both day and night. It needs considerable fuel energy to keep the plant in green leaf: for it is not allowed to defoliate, as with normal winter care, although a few leaves will naturally drop. Careful watering will be required to obtain the ideal soil condition, a slight dampness. The plant is restful, neither dormant nor entirely active.

With the improved light around early February, plants take on a completely different look and are ready to be potted-back (repotted). Those in 5in (12.5cm) pots are potted-back to 4in (10cm) pots, whilst those in 4in (10cm) pots go back to either 3in (7.5cm) or 3¼in (9cm) pots. Any compost needed must of course be new. The biennial plant now has plenty of new white roots, when compared with normal overwintered plants. Careful handling is needed when potting-back to ensure these new roots are not lost or damaged. Some growers pot *on* at the specified time of early February, rather than potting *back*. For myself, I find the potting-back method more successful.

After potting-back or potting-on, the plants are then cultivated as with any other growing method, with the usual spring and early summer potting-on programme, 1in (2.5cm) at a time. The normal feeding programme commences immediately the plants have recovered from any check, mainly using a feed with a high nitrogen content.

The stopping procedure is exactly the same as with other methods of training, allowing 60 days for singles and 80 days for doubles; stop after every two pairs of leaves, although most successful exhibitors, especially with the shrub or bush shape, stop after every one pair of leaves. Shapes other than the shrub or bush, such as standards, baskets and trailers, can of course also be trained with the biennial method.

The short-jointed cultivars are particularly suitable for the biennial method, in final pots of 6in (15cm). I suggest Border Queen, or its sister seedling Eden Lady; Cambridge Louie; Celia Smedley – not quite so short-jointed as some; Countess of Aberdeen; Cloverdale Pearl; Display; Dusky Beauty; General Monk; Heidi Ann; Lady Isobel Barnett; Lena Dalton; Lindisfarne; Margaret Roe; Mieke Meursing; Mr A. Huggett; Nellie Nuttall; Pacquesa; Pink Darling; President Leo Boullemier; Snowcap; Tom Thumb; and White Joy. If stopped hard these will have huge, tight heads. The plants grow extremely large so you may have to restrict the number grown.

Staking
Staking and tying is permitted on show plants if unobtrusive. Position any necessary supports early, especially any central stake, so that the growth can come up around them.

Bushes and Shrubs

Bush and shrub fuchsias are the easiest to train. All aspects of cultivation are basically the same for the bush and the shrub. The British Fuchsia Society, although differentiating between the two, does not schedule different classes for each specific type. Its definition of a bush is that it has a maximum 1½in (3.75cm) of clear stem to indicate the presence of a single plant. The shrub is defined as a plant with shrubby growth, having several shoots produced from below soil level. There are recognised shapes of bush or shrub: they should not be like Topsy who 'just growed', although a few naturally self-branching cultivars will make good plants with little attention.

To reach the showbench with evenly balanced plants, you have to give some detailed attention during the training period. Choose a fairly vigorous type of cultivar raised as an early spring cutting, or a cutting struck in the autumn and kept in green leaf during the winter. The time to start any training – not only bush training – is when the cutting has made both good root and good top growth while in its first or second pot, usually either the 2in (5cm) or 3in (7.5cm) size.

When the plant has developed three pairs of leaves, remove the centre growing-tip – the first stop or pinch. This encourages side-shoots left on the plants to grow outward. When these have made two pairs of leaves, they are stopped. Instead of having just one shoot, you now have six. From these resultant six side-shoots, all of which will break again, the tips are again pinched at a further two pairs of leaves; this is your second stop, and you now have not six but twenty-four shoots.

For normal decorative use, these two stops are usually sufficient, but for large specimens for the showbench, the stopping procedure can continue until you are satisfied. Successful exhibitors, particularly when growing on the biennial method, stop their plants – after the initial stopping – at every pair of leaves, an operation

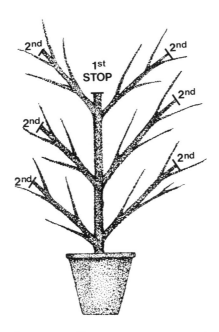

Bush training. Stop at three pairs of leaves, stop again at each two pairs. This will give twenty-four side-shoots

carried out many times, until the ultimate size of the plant is reached. It is emphasised that each stopping made delays flowering by approximately two months. Full details for stopping are given in the section on this subject. When you do your stopping, *all shoots must be stopped at the same time*, otherwise you will have half a plant in flower and the other half in leaf or small-bud stage – no use for the showbench. When the growing-tip is large enough, use finger and thumb and remove the tip completely, without leaving jagged pieces or damaging the young tender shoots left in the axils.

Every pinching delays flowering but increases the size of the plant. A specimen bush or shrub plant ready for the bench in its 6in (15cm) pot should measure some $2\frac{1}{2}$ft (75cm) across. Two dream plants for the exhibitor in this context are Border Queen and Cloverdale Pearl, which both produce extremely vigorous growth, are close-jointed and easy to train into almost perfect symmetrical shapes. However, no two cultivars are exactly the same, and stopping times quoted are not exact; you have to learn by experience. Many are early-flowering (such as La Campanella and Red Spider); latecomers include Mission Bells, Peppermint Stick and Winston Churchill.

Exhibition specimen plant of White Joy in a 6in (15cm) pot

While the cutting is in its first and second pots I recommend John Innes No 1 if a reliable one is available; if not, a proprietary soilless compost. Keep your plants growing steadily by repeated moves to pots of gradually increasing size, from 3in (7.5cm) to 4in (10cm). At this stage you can move on to John Innes No 2 and remain with that, or else carry on with soilless compost when moving from 4in (10cm) to 5in (12.5cm) and from 5in (12.5cm) to 6in (15cm) pots. On current growth a 5in (12.5cm) pot will be large enough for the first year, but with vigorous cultivars it may be possible to finalise in a 6in (15cm). At every potting-on, protect the plants from excessive sunlight; water-in well and place them in the shadiest part of the greenhouse for 2 or 3 days – under the staging is ideal.

Avoid encouraging soft growth – long shoots or stems that will not carry the weight of blooms without bending or snapping. Control greenhouse temperature and give full ventilation on all suitable occasions, and also carefully space out the plants. They must never touch one another. Remember the 'turning routine': every pot should be revolved half a turn every third day, because a well-grown bush or shrub plant must be symmetrical, with even growth, when viewed from any angle.

Suitable cultivars are detailed in the section on training under the biennial method (page 24) and the section on cultivars for different purposes (page 59).

Shrub Judging Criteria
A shrub fuchsia has the quality of being shrubby, ie it produces shoots from below soil level in addition to having a main trunk with lateral growths. It should be grown freely but with a little judicious training to obtain a balanced plant. An abundance of foliage and flower is wanted over the entire plant, according to variety, viewed from all sides and the top. The size of plant and container should be in proportion.

Cultural proficiency: Cultural proficiency will be assessed by the abundance of vigorous symmetrical growth; it should have received but little formal training to become a balanced plant, with overall quality and freshness, and that full coverage of foliage and flower, according to variety, over the entire plant, top to bottom. No special shape or form is required, other than good balance being apparent when the plant is seen from all sides.

Bush Judging Criteria
A bush plant is developed on a short stem free of all growth for a maximum of $1\frac{1}{2}$in (3.75cm), so that a single plant is clearly indicated. The entire plant should be covered with an abundance of foliage and flower, according to variety, and as with a shrub fuchsia you must have a balanced symmetrical plant from any angle. The plant must be in proportion to container size.

Cultural proficiency: Cultural proficiency is assessed on the overall quality of growth, on the uniformity and fullness of growth when viewed from all sides. Foliage should be abundant and clean, over the entire body of the plant. Stakes, if used, should be limited.

Standards

Having achieved reasonable success with exhibiting bush and shrub plants, the exhibitor usually next attempts a standard. Standards are in fact bush or shrub plants growing on a stem of desired length. For exhibition purposes a maximum and minimum length of clear stem is stipulated. The British Fuchsia Society defines the length of clear stem required from soil level to the lowest branch. (The level of the first branch is the point at which the branch joins the main stem.)

Clear stem from 5in (13cm) to 10in (25.5cm) for miniature standards

Clear stem from 12in (30cm) to 18in (45cm) for quarter-standards

Clear stem from 18in (45cm) to 30in (75cm) for half-standards

Clear stem from 30in (75cm) to 42in (107cm) for full standards

It is possible to produce a small specimen standard, especially a miniature, in the first year, but to obtain a good specimen the period of training needed is some eighteen to twenty-four months. Start growth in early spring, or during the months of June to August on the biennial method. The former method works all right, as spring, summer and autumn provide sufficient time for the plant to become established before, if necessary, resting for the winter. A much better and quicker specimen, however, will be obtained if sufficient heat is available during the winter for the maintenance of growth in full green leaf – which is in effect an adapted biennial method. However, with the orthodox biennial method it may not be possible to attain the desired height, especially with a full standard, before the winter, and a temperature of 45°F (7.2°C) will be required throughout the dreary months to maintain unchecked growth. The standard will be completed during the following late spring and summer.

Select the early green tip-cutting of a strong upright cultivar such as Celia Smedley or Snowcap; or if you decide upon a weeping standard, use a cultivar like Marinka, or any vigorous but lax American cultivar. Some cultivars such as Snowcap or Mephisto often throw three shoots, and occasionally four shoots, in the leaf axil, instead of the normal two; if you are fortunate and can select these, then an even better and bigger head will ultimately result. The cutting is grown on unchecked without stopping, from the initial 2in (5cm) pot stage until it is large enough to be transferred to its second pot, 3in (7.5cm).

It should then have made sufficient growth to need early support. This is important; when the young, unstopped plant has made around 6in (15cm) of stem, insert a thin cane fairly close to the stem and tie not too loosely at intervals of 2in (5cm) throughout the whole period of training, until the desired height is achieved. Although a tedious operation, this constant tying ensures a straight stem, the hallmark of a good standard. Whilst the plant is making both height and rapid growth, remember to revolve it a half-turn every third day.

While growth takes place, all the side-shoots in the leaf axil are

Early stages of training a standard. Side-shoots have been removed from the leaf axils on the lower part of the plant, and the stem is being tied to a support every 2in (5cm)

removed (rubbed out); but, and this again is important, the leaves are retained. They are not removed until the intended height and the head have almost been made, as the plant needs them. When removing the side-shoots, *always* leave the uppermost two or three pairs of shoots on the stem.

The object is to obtain very rapid and unchecked growth. Achieve it by constant potting-on, increasing the size of the pot 1in (2.5cm) at a time, and by giving a high-nitrogen feed. At this stage pay constant attention to the roots; as soon as they have worked themselves around the rootball, the plant must be moved into its next pot. Should the plant become pot-bound, it will have the normal tendency to bud and flower: this must be avoided whilst the attaining of the intended height goes on. To counteract it I do over-pot slightly with the very vigorous cultivars, using a 4in (10cm) pot when the young plant is approximately 8 to 9in (20 to 23cm) high; when the young whip, as it is now called, has reached 12in (30.5cm), it is moved on to a 5in (12.5cm) pot. Should the plant develop either buds or flowers, then upright growth is retarded or will cease; the removal of buds and flowers becomes absolutely necessary, and then acts as a stop, with the loss of a shoot in the immediate future.

The ultimate final pot size should be 5in (12.5cm) for miniature, 6in (15cm) for quarter, 7 or 8in (18 or 20cm) for half and 8in (20cm) or even larger for full standards.

Feeding can commence with a weak nitrogenous feed, when the plant is established in the 3in (7.5cm) pot stage, and then be continued throughout the training period. This will also assist in the required rapid growth. Continue with the removal of side-shoots, and when potting-on always increase the length of cane or support to about 6in (15cm) to 12in (30.5cm) above the achieved height. Make sure that ties never cut into the stem.

When the desired length of stem is made, grow on until four pairs of leaves have developed above it. These are retained to develop into the head – or in other words into the bush or shrub at the top of your long stem. Now make your definite stop by removing the leader, or the uppermost terminal shoot. The ideal number of side-shoots left at the top would be four pairs, although six is acceptable. These are now left to grow, exactly as on a bush or shrub plant. The pinching and stopping procedure is to stop at each two pairs of leaves; usually three or four stops are necessary to achieve a well-developed head. Should you require a very tight head, then stop after each pair of leaves after the initial stopping of two pairs.

When everything has been achieved and the plant is in full bloom, the depth of the head should be approximately one-third of the stem height, and the width about two-thirds of the height.

When considering winter care for standards, create a slightly higher temperature for resting purposes, 38°F (3.3°C) to 40°F (4.4°C),

(*top left*) Yuletide, a fascinating American double, similar to Swingtime but with even larger blooms and stiffer growth. Excellent exhibition cultivar (*Author*)

(*top right*) F. denticulata, an excellent species for the showbench, with strong upright growth. Reddish-pink tube and sepals are tipped green, with a red corolla. Flowers rather late and likes a little heat. Also known as *F. serratifolia* (*Dr S. Appel*)

(*below*) Harry Gray, one of the best and most recent trailers, shown to perfection in an exhibition hanging pot. Double rose-pink and white, best described as a white Marinka. Makes a wonderful basket (*Author*)

as all tall methods of training leave the plants more susceptible to frost than smaller types of growth. Pruning should be done hard, in the earlier months of the year; this prevents bare spaces, the 'room for birds to nest in' that is too often seen.

Standards should be repotted (potted back), and then started into growth for a full season's normal cultivation. However, when standards are established in their final pots of 8in (20cm) or over, it may not be necessary to pot back but only to remove as much as possible of the old spent soil, especially on the top, and replace it with fresh compost in the existing-size (or slightly larger) pots.

Standards are in their prime during their third and fourth years. After that time they make heavy wood and are reluctant to break low down on the framework of the head.

Standards Judging Criteria
The trunk shall be straight and clear, free of knots or other ugly blemishes, and may be supported by a stake of a proportionate size. The total head should be a profusion of branches, presenting a full and balanced effect of lush foliage and flowers, according to cultivar, over the entire head with no gaps. The plant should be in proportion to the container size.

Cultural proficiency: This will be assessed on the overall quality of plant growth. Uniformity and fullness of growth should be apparent when viewed from all sides, and the plant must be well furnished with clean foliage and flowers, according to cultivar. It must present a well-balanced effect. The stem should be straight and true, free of blemishes caused by the removal of laterals.

Suitable cultivars for the training of standards are included in the section on cultivars for different purposes (page 59).

Miniature Standards

This type of training really belongs to the small pot culture definition now included in most show schedules. The miniature is smaller than the quarter-standard, but easier and quicker to train

(*top*) Coachman, grown as a superb half-basket. Old British introduction of pale salmon and rich orange-vermilion. Very free flowering and early, with beautiful clear colouring (*Author*)

(*below*) Lady Kathleen Spence, the only cultivar to receive the British Fuchsia Society Gold Medal Certificate. Delicate pastel-coloured single, which gives its best colour when shaded. Good as basket or trailer (*S. J. Wilson*)

than orthodox standards. For show purposes the pot size is restricted to 5in (12.5cm), and the maximum length of clear stem is restricted to 10in (25.5cm) from soil level to the first branch. These measurements ensure a standard of balanced proportions.

For miniatures the selection of suitable cultivars is vital. Cultivars such as Swingtime or Royal Velvet have blooms that would be completely out of character with the size of the head wanted and the overall balance. Concentrate upon the smaller-flowered cultivars, such as Bobby Wingrove; Christmas Elf; Cloverdale Jewel; Curly Q; Derby Imp; Joan's Delight; Little Beauty; Minirose; Northway; Papoose; Ravensbarrow; Son of Thumb; Tsjiep (pronounced Chips) – a new outstanding Dutch introduction; Tom Woods; and Westminster Chimes.

With careful cultivation it is possible to create miniature weeping standards, using the small-flowered trailing cultivars – Auntie Jinks; Baby Chang (a real miniature); Daisy Bell; La Campanella; Mantilla; or President Margaret Slater – identical to Cascade, except for having smaller flowers. Mini-standards can be achieved on one season's growth, known as current growth. An early spring cutting makes excellent material, although a second-year plant is the ideal. The cutting is grown on unchecked without stopping from its initial 2in (5cm) pot. Cultivation from now on is exactly as described in the previous section for orthodox standards. The only variation could be just before the desired height is achieved, making sure of having at least three pairs of shoots available to form the head. For mini-standards, four pairs of shoots would be sufficient for a proportional head.

Besides miniature standards, small pot culture can be extended to other types of training: conicals, pillars, fans, espaliers and even pyramids.

Judging Criteria for Small Pot Culture
These criteria are for all forms of training under small pot culture. The true proportions of the plant form will be expected, and good foliage and flowers, typical in size, form and colour for the plant exhibited. The relative difficulty of the plant form chosen will be given full consideration.

Pyramids, conicals, pillars, espaliers and fans, when grown in small pot culture, will be allowed a maximum of 20in (60cm) height, soil level to apex, with a maximum pot size of 5in (12.5cm). Baskets will be a maximum of 6in (16.5cm) diameter.

Basket Cultivation

This method of training allows the fuchsia to be seen from its best angle, at eye-level. Plant growth should fill the centre and top, continuing to surge over the edge in a sweeping cascade effect. Growth should be uniform, with clean foliage and an abundance of bloom, which when the plant is exhibited must obscure the whole basket.

Although any size basket can be used by the home gardener, the British Fuchsia Society, to obtain some degree of uniformity, limits the size to a maximum diameter of 15in (38cm) for the full basket and a maximum 14in (35cm) for the half-basket, measured across the back. Its present schedules stipulate that the full basket must be of hemispherical shape, and the half-basket demi-hemispherical – straight-sided baskets are not permitted. This may be revised in the future.

Baskets can be of various sizes and materials. Use round baskets measuring between 10in (25.5cm) and 15in (38cm), preferably the galvanised-wire type, which are much stronger and hold their shape better than the modern plastic-covered baskets. Half-baskets are either 12in (30cm) or 14in (35cm). All these sizes are within the maximum measurements allowed for show.

Planting five plants from 3¼in (8.5cm) pots into a 14in (35cm) basket in late March

The ideal time for planting is late March and very early April, especially with July shows in mind: a fairly long period of growth is needed to produce long, healthy, trailing stems. My long experience has convinced me that baskets are much better grown on current growth, starting with new plants each year. That is not to say that excellent baskets cannot be grown with two-year-old plants, and older too.

It is better to plant one type of cultivar, not to mix, as growth, balance and flowering are more easily controlled. Put three plants into a 10in (25.5cm) basket, three or four into a 12in (30cm) basket and five or six into a 15in (38cm) basket. With the half-baskets, the 12in (30cm) size will only accommodate two plants, from 3¼in (8.5cm) pots. The 14in (35cm) will usually take three of these.

The list of suitable cultivars to use is lengthy – virtually anything that trails, and for the half-baskets anything that trails or is of lax habit. Although Marinka and La Campanella may be automatic choices, others include Red Spider; Harry Gray; Pink Galore; Jack Acland; and President Stanley Wilson. In the half-basket class, Swingtime and Coachman, together with Jack Shahan and Mrs W. Rundle, are excellent choices.

Showmen often grow them on the biennial method rather than on current growth. To obtain the finest results use plants produced from autumn-struck cuttings. If these are not available, select plants grown from early spring tip-cuttings. If your own plants are not early enough, obtain some from a specialist nurseryman, preferably in 3in (7.5cm) pots. Stop after three pairs of leaves. From then on, pinch out at every resultant three pairs of leaves; this ensures those long trailing laterals. After the third or fourth pinching, you need all the patience in the world, the hundreds – not scores – of pinches taking considerable time.

For the actual planting, the round bottom is a great inconvenience; half-baskets are even worse, and I treat them in pairs. Place your basket in a very large flower pot of around 10in (25.5cm) size, or a suitable bucket; this will give you complete control. Line the basket with moss, if obtainable; sphagnum moss is superior, but failing this any moss will do. Modern peat liners or polythene sheeting are alternatives, but they should be pierced liberally to ensure good drainage. The polythene lining greatly assists in conserving moisture, avoiding excessive drying out in hot conditions and reducing the watering needed.

Then almost fill the basket with either John Innes No 2 compost or soilless compost, having previously placed a fair quantity of

Freshly planted basket, showing special iron stand for transporting

President Stanley Wilson, one of the most floriferous of basket cultivars – a single, with carmine tube and sepals and rose-carmine corolla. Shown here as a half-basket

sphagnum peat on the bottom. Do not insert the plants vertically, but at an angle of 45° around the edge of the basket, already giving a slightly trailing position. This leaves a space in the middle, but unless you are using cultivars with a thin wiry growth, such as La Campanella or Lakeside, do not worry; they will soon spread and cover the whole basket. With the two cultivars named I do plant one in the middle to obtain better balance.

Finish filling the basket with the compost, firmly planting with finger pressure, and leave the top with a saucer-shaped depression for watering purposes. Water well with a fine-rosed can, place the basket in a shady position for three or four days, and then bring it out for hanging in its final position. Hanging baskets when watered are heavy, so never suspend them from sash-bars, and if hung from the rafters make sure the structure will bear the weight. Remember your turning procedure, to obtain uniformity of growth. During warm weather take the baskets down and soak them in a bucket – soaking both base and compost.

Judging Criteria for Baskets
An optional number of plants are to be grown in a wire or plastic basket, to be viewed from top and sides when displayed in an elevated position. Plant growth must fill the centre and top of the basket and continue to surge over the edge in a sweeping cascade. Uniform growth, clean leaf and an abundance of flower, according to variety, must continue to at least the depth of the container and should be evenly distributed from the crown to the end of the trailing growths. The container itself should not be visible when viewed from eye-level. The size of the basket must not exceed that stated in the schedule. And if the show schedule states 'hemi-spherical' or 'demi-hemispherical', a straight-sided basket is not allowed.

Hanging Pots

Baskets, especially of the larger sizes, occupy more space than some growers can offer. They are also difficult to transport. Over recent years a new method of growing and exhibiting has emerged: the hanging pot or container. The British Fuchsia Society does not yet have classes for these, but most local societies now include in their schedules 'one plant in hanging pot not exceeding 6in (15cm)', or 'not exceeding 8in (20cm)'.

The convenience of using plastic pots, in a decorous green,

with three hanger-stays, is obvious, both for exhibiting and for transportation. The best pots of this kind I have found are marketed by BEF Products (Essex) Ltd, of Billericay, Essex.

Many growers seem to use the wrong cultivars for hanging pots, selecting either large-flowering doubles or stiff upright varieties. Another fault is choosing cultivars that grow too far outward from the pot. My ideal plant would be one trained as near as possible to the shape of a ball of flowers, with the container completely hidden. Try to grow a plant in proportion to the size of the container; an enormous plant in a small pot, or a small plant with few laterals, looks completely wrong. Select cultivars of a trailing or lax habit, and preferably with small or medium-sized flowers. You need, if possible, a self-branching cultivar providing plenty of growth without too many stops. The following is a selection of cultivars that from my own experience are the most suitable for hanging pots. Asterisks indicate those that are best of all for this purpose:

*Barry's Queen (synonymous with Golden Border Queen); Border Queen; Cascade; Cambridge Louie (with weights); Daisy Bell; Derby Imp; Harry Gray; Iris Amer (with weights); Jack Shahan; La Campanella; Lena; Marinka; President Stanley Wilson; *Princessita; Walsingham; and *Westminster Chimes.

An early spring cutting gradually potted on through the 3in (7.5cm) and 4in (10cm) sizes, or even to 5in (12.5cm), could be successfully flowered on current growth. But I consider a second-year plant is better. When using a second-year plant, choose one pruned and repotted (potted back) by February in a 3½in (9cm) pot. Continue with normal spring cultivation by potting on, through to 4in (10cm) and 5in (12.5cm) pots, stopping and pinching when necessary and remembering initial feeding.

By May, the plant should be ready for its final hanging pot or container, whether raised by current-growth method or the alternative. This is the time to insert the plastic hanging-stays, so that the plant may grow around the pot and hangers. By the middle of July you will have a riot of colour. Your emphasis is now on feeding.

Cut Blooms

The majority of show schedules, national and local, include a class calling for 'six cut blooms to be displayed on boards provided'. The fuchsia pedicel is quite short and the boards provided include water tubes in which the flowers are inserted with the flower uppermost. When exhibiting, take care over the size of the flowers; they should be typical of the cultivar: neither too large nor too small. Flowers should be perfect – any blooms premature in opening (the most common fault), bruised or faded will lose points.

The perfect bloom is one typical of its variety, carrying just enough pollen on the stigma to attract pollinating insects. It may be some help to remind you that a fuchsia bloom lasts ten days from opening, and pollen breaks after the fifth day. After premature flowers, the next most common faults in these classes are flowers that are much too small and not typical, and flowers having more, or less, than four sepals. To obtain complete freshness, which is essential, the flowers must be gathered and staged a few hours before judging. Staging overnight before the show is a waste of energy.

5 Training Large Structures

In training fuchsias into any of the structures such as conicals, pillars, pyramids, espaliers and fans, general principles apply, irrespective of shape or size. The selection of the correct type of cultivar is of paramount importance. A long period of growth is essential, little being achieved in the first year; three or even four years are required for a completed specimen. But it should be grown as quickly as possible, requiring high-nitrogen feeding and not much potash during training. All large structures are in their prime much later than the smaller forms of fuchsia plants, possibly after as much as eight years. They all need adequate support in the early stages of training. But try not to have to replace heavy stakes and supports, as you can cause considerable root damage.

Do not attempt large structures unless you have considerable space available, especially for overwintering. The top growth of any cultivar, whether classified as hardy or not, will not survive out of doors in winter in Britain, in any type of container. Before growing for exhibition, remember the size of your greenhouse and the problems of subsequent removal, and the need of spacious transport for carrying specimens to shows.

Conicals

A form associated with the late-Victorian era, often confused, even by experienced growers, with the pyramid. The conical is a much quicker and easier method of training, achieving a similar shape.

For exhibition purposes the growth should be not less than 4ft (120cm) tall, from soil level, as opposed to the lower height of the small pot culture. The shape is similar to the pyramid but more gradual; width at base should be no less than 2ft (60cm), with the top tapering more finely than the pyramid. When fully grown, the completed plant should be trained to a height of 6ft (180cm), and with correct balance; the base width should be approximately 3ft (90cm).

When starting, select a vigorous upright cultivar as early as possible from a spring-struck cutting. It is essential to select one which will produce plenty of side-shoots, preferably self-branching, such as Fascination; Mrs Lovell Swisher; Display; Constance; Border Queen; Checkerboard; or Phyllis. The plant is allowed to grow unchecked and unstopped on a single stem, right from the early pot. When established, preferably in its 3in (8.5cm) pot, root-prune by removing the tap root.

From now on, grow on without the slightest check, using the gradual potting-on method with regular high-nitrogen feed. Do not allow the plant to become pot-bound, as that leads to premature flowering, which will retard upright growth. Insert your cane as early as possible. When you pot on into large pots, always use a cane larger than the main stem.

All side-shoots are allowed to develop naturally. The lowest or the first shoots should be stopped at three pairs of leaves, and the side-shoots which develop on the middle of the main stem are

Conical training

stopped at two pairs; the uppermost side-shoots are stopped after one pair of leaves. Any resultant shoots from any of these stops can be stopped at two pairs of leaves, or if tight growth is desired, at one pair of leaves, according to choice – to control the tapered shape of the conical. Growth should be *rapid*. With good feeding and correct environment, a height of 5ft (150cm) can be made in the first year. By this time the plant should be in the 6in (15cm) pot. Turn the plant frequently, for uniformity of growth, and give plenty of space and headroom around it.

Judging Criteria for Conicals

Conical structures can be grown and exhibited either as a single plant or a multiple-plant structure, using a maximum of three plants in the same container where the schedule so specifies.

A single-plant conical must have been grown to produce a finely tapering structure. It differs from a pyramid in that the lower section is reduced in circumference, the plant being tall and slender, tapering gradually and gracefully to a fine apex. A short stem free of growth is shown, in order to indicate clearly that it is a single plant. It should be covered with good foliage and flower, according to cultivar. Plant size is unrestricted, but the plant must be in proportion to its container.

Cultural proficiency: This will be assessed on the degree of skill shown in developing the uniform structure into a true conical growth. From a single plant a gradual taper must be maintained from bottom to apex and must be constant around the circumference. Good foliage and flowers are needed in overall quantity to achieve a well-balanced slender and elegant plant, in proportion to its container size.

For multiple-plant conicals the judging criteria are similar. Three plants are used; their main stems should be in close proximity and tied to a centre stake. Through the use of multiple plants, height and diameter will be larger and a greater volume of flower and foliage will be expected.

Pillars

The late James Lye was a master at training this type of growth. Photographs record specimen plants several feet high and 3ft (90cm) across. Many of his cultivars are ideal for pillar training. The idea is to produce two stems at different heights, with uniform growth the whole way up, and to prevent any tapering at the top.

There are two methods of training pillars. The first is to use a single plant, and after its first stopping at two pairs of leaves, allow the strongest of each pair to grow – one as a bush plant and the other as a standard. The remaining weaker shoots are rubbed out. The other method is to use two plants in the same pot, one plant trained as a standard and the other as a bush.

Before the new judging criteria by the British Fuchsia Society, plants grown for exhibition were permitted to have one stem only. Present regulations permit multiple stems, and these cultural instructions concentrate on the two-plant method; it is easier and also produces quicker results. Furthermore it avoids initial checks and, most important, produces much more even growth.

Select two identical vigorous cuttings of cultivars such as Barbara;

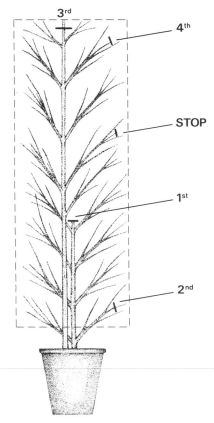

Pillar training by the two-plant method; one plant trained as a standard, the other as a bush

Fascination; Joan Smith; Jack Shahan; Muriel; Snowcap; or a vigorous cultivar by Lye. Take them as early as possible in the spring. Grow one as a bush, stopping at three pairs of leaves, the other as a standard without any stopping. At this stage they will be growing in their second pots of 3in (7.5cm) or 3¼in (8.5cm); when well established, root prune by removing the tap root, which is essential for this type of training. When ready for potting on, instead of potting singly, pot both plants together, side by side, into a 5in (12.5cm) pot – a clay pot preferably, with loam-based compost. At this early stage provide a suitable cane or support, common to both plants.

Should you desire your pillar to attain an ultimate height of 5ft (150cm), your aim is to grow and flower the bush plant to a height of 30in (75cm), and the standard from that height of 30in to the top. Keep the stems close together during subsequent growth. The bush plant must be stopped at three pairs of leaves and again stopped after these resultant side-shoots have made two further pairs of leaves. Make further stops as necessary, so that all shoots are even in length.

Whilst all this growth takes place, the standard plant is grown with all side-shoots in the leaf axils removed, until it reaches just beyond the 30in (75cm) height. When this has been attained, all side-shoots are retained and the plant is stopped at 5ft (150cm). The procedure then is to stop these side-shoots after two pairs of leaves, to develop the head or the top half of the plant.

Judging Criteria for Pillars
Two or three plants of the same cultivar go into the pillar. The main items must be closely adjacent and tied neatly to a central stake. It is expected that multiple-plant pillars will have a larger height and diameter than single-plant pillars. The relation of diameter to height must be regulated to present a tall graceful pillar of foliage and flower. Width or diameter has to remain constant from bottom to top. The plant should be in good proportion to its container size. The judging criteria for single-plant pillars are exactly the same, except that a short section of bare stem from soil level to the first laterals must be shown to indicate clearly the single-plant structure.

Pyramids

This method of training demands the grower's greatest skill. The term 'pyramid' is self-explanatory: growth should be uniformly tapering, from pot level to apex. Many growers, however, confuse the pyramid with the conical, a much easier method of training. The finished pyramid should be not less than 4ft (120cm) tall, with its width at the base not less than 3ft (90cm). Although the new British Fuchsia Society judging regulations allow the use of more than one plant, I cannot visualise the advantage of doing so, considering the pyramid can only be achieved by careful and skilful manipulation upon a single stem.

For pyramids, select a very strong, vigorous and upright cultivar such as Brutus; Display; Pink Darling; Achievement; Celia Smedley; or any of the vigorous Lye's cultivars – Amy Lye, Clipper or Lye's Unique. When selecting, use a young plant grown from an early green tip-cutting, looking for the three-leaf variety instead of the normal two. Root prune as early as possible, by removing the tap root and so allowing the feeder roots to develop more strongly. While the plant is in its 3in (7.5cm) or 3¼in (8.5cm) pot, allow the growth to reach 9 or 10in (23 or 25.5cm) before the first stopping. The result will usually be that you have three or four pairs of leaves left in the leaf axils. From these breaks, only one, the most vigorous at the top, is selected to form the new leader; the other shoot is rubbed out. The plant must be kept in constant growth throughout the whole training period, and not bud or flower prematurely. This can be prevented by the gradual potting-on procedure. Once the plant has attained moderate growth, feed regularly with a high-nitrogen fertiliser, ensuring rapid growth and height.

At the time of the first stopping, give a stout support to your main central stem, which must always be above the height at the growing leader. The first stopping will induce the side-shoots to develop, and these are stopped after three pairs of leaves. Make all stops at the same time to ensure even growth. Further side-shoots will develop, and these in turn are stopped at a further two pairs of leaves.

The plant is now probably in its 5in (12.5cm) pot. The framework to support this growth may be temporary, but it must be strong enough to support the growth from the side-shoots; to achieve this insert canes at an angle around the edge of the pot. Tie one or two canes horizontally to the main stem, and tie the side-shoots to these. The new leader must be stopped for the second time, after another three or four pairs of leaves have developed: once again take the more vigorous shoot of the uppermost pair, rubbing out the one not required. The other remaining shoots should be encouraged to train outwards for the second set of horizontal laterals; stop them after they have made three pairs of leaves, then again after two pairs.

After this stage when more growth has been made, you again select a new leader, the more vigorous of the top pair of shoots, rubbing out the one not required. The whole process is repeated as many times as needed, until the desired height is achieved. The essential point to watch during the stopping programme is that you stop the side-shoots and the leader *alternately*; and again, always make sure that when side-shoots are stopped they are all stopped at the same time, unnecessary shoots being rubbed out to avoid overcrowding.

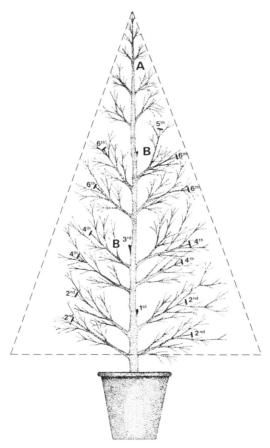

Pyramid training, showing leader (A), rubbed-out shoots (B), plus 1st, 2nd, 3rd, 4th, 5th and 6th stops

Mention must be made of the training of the lower side-shoots. During the early stages of growth, naturally the longest, it will be necessary to train them somewhat vertically upon the temporary framework. Do not attempt at this time to train them horizontally, as this would result in checking growth. When buds and flowers together with the normal branches appear, they will fall into position, much as trailing branches bend under the weight of flowers in hanging baskets.

The finished specimen must be symmetrical, so turn it regularly. After three or four years it should be up to 8 or 10ft (244 to 305cm) high, the final pot size being approximately 10 or 12in (25.5 or 30cm).

Judging Criteria for Pyramids
A single plant developed to produce a structure tapering uniformly from bottom to top. The pyramid shape must be apparent from all sides. A short trunk must be shown to indicate clearly the single-plant structure. The relation of the height to the diameter of the lowest section should be that of a tall tapering tree, and in proportion to the container size. The plant should be fully covered with foliage and flower overall. A central stake is allowed.

Espaliers and Fans

Although little seen these days, espalier fuchsias create flattering amazement. Espaliers can be trained as horizontal or fan; they are intended to be viewed from the front. The finished specimen should be well furnished with fresh blooms and clean foliage, and although there is no restriction in size, the plant should be of balanced growth (and of a size you can move in and out of your greenhouse!).

Choose your cultivar with care. This type of training needs vigorous growth that is also lax – not trailing, yet the flowers must cascade. Possible cultivars include Miss California; Jack Shahan; Swingtime; Kathy Louise; Muriel; Lena, White Spider. The

(*top*) Border Queen, a popular and successful showbench banker, grown on the biennial method. Neyson-rose and amethyst-violet, flushed pink. This single flowering cultivar always comes true (*Author*)

(*below*) Cascade, a typical exhibition basket variety which blooms profusely, with true single flowers, very pendulous and cascading. The white tube and sepals are heavily flushed carmine, with deep carmine corolla (*S. J. Wilson*)

objective is to produce a plant with a central upright stem, with a series of four, five or six branches, equidistant from one another, coming from the stem at an angle of 45° for the fan, and at right angles for the horizontal. The ultimate height of the plant should be 5 to 6ft (150 to 182cm) although there is no restriction upon the height or the number of laterals produced. Grow to as many laterals as nearly opposed to each other as possible.

Start with a plant grown from an early green tip-cutting, allowing it to grow unstopped and with some means of central support. Root prune, as when growing the other large structures, by removing the tap root when the plant has reached the 3in (7.5cm) pot stage; again we require vigorous growth with as many feeder roots as possible. Obtain the rapid growth by the usual gradual potting-on and high-nitrogen feeding, remembering to rub out any undesired side-shoots which might upset the balance of the finished specimen. Insert a stronger cane at the second potting-on stage. For the ultimate framework support, use a square stake with holes drilled in it, inserting round canes the length of the laterals to act as supports. When the desired height has been made, the plant is stopped and the supports for the laterals are put in where these branches will eventually grow.

The laterals are allowed to grow along the framework un-checked, without any stopping, until they reach the required width; never stop them until then, and make suitable ties all along the supports. Always tie the laterals on the top of the supports so that the ultimate growth will hide them. With espalier training, try to obtain tight or close growth; to achieve this, all side-shoots on the laterals should be stopped after each pair of leaves. The resultant shoots from this stopping should also be stopped after a further one pair of leaves has been made.

Judging Criteria for Espaliers

Espaliers and fans are single plants trained on a latticed structure. The laterals should be matched symmetrically on each side of the plant centre. Espaliers should have horizontally trained laterals and fans should have laterals trained into a fan design. Whether the

(*top*) Iceberg, a fine example of an exhibition standard. Almost an all-white single except for red-tipped tube and slightly red veining. As with all-whites, colour develops best under shade (*Author*)

(*below*) Author's greenhouse in full flower in August. Note the adequate shading (*Author*)

Espalier training (horizontal)

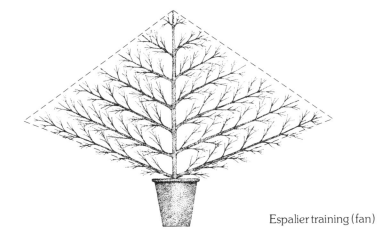

Espalier training (fan)

structural design originates from a central trunk, extending the entire height of the plant, or from a chosen number of basic laterals, a short trunk consistent with the overall plant size or development must be shown free of all growth, to indicate the single-plant structure. All laterals must be fully covered with foliage and flowers, according to cultivar. The plant must be in good proportion to the size of the container, viewed from the front.

Cultural proficiency: The basic factor for an espalier or fan is your skill in developing the chosen design into an arranged balance of symmetrically matched laterals on both sides of the plant centre. Although grown for frontal effect, the rear of the latticed structure should be well covered with good clean foliage. All laterals must be fully covered with foliage and flowers.

6 Ornamental, Variegated, Species and Triphyllas

Ornamental and Variegated

Confusion can occur among both exhibitors and judges who do not clearly understand just what constitutes ornamental or variegated foliage, in classes that call for them.

Although the British Fuchsia Society does not lay down any definition, it is generally accepted that 'variegated' foliage must have two or more distinct colours. Typical examples are Autumnale, with its golden and coppery-red leaves changing to dark red and salmon, mahogany and russet, and Golden Marinka, with attractive cream edges and patches on a medium yellow or green leaf.

'Ornamental' is not so easily defined. Cultivars with ornamental foliage are those grown for their foliage beauty, and they include cultivars with foliage that is distinctly yellow, usually described as golden, and sometimes with red veining. Examples of ornamentals are cultivars with lime-green or yellow-green leaves, or leaves with a blush or overlay of a second colour, such as Golden Treasure and Cloth of Gold. The cultivar President falls into the group with blush overlay, having a reddened or bronzed addition to a basic green leaf; it is a typical ornamental cultivar that can lose its ornamental value with maturity or incorrect conditions.

Red-veined foliage is not recognised as ornamental or variegated unless some additional characteristics are present. Most ornamental and variegated cultivars are not free-flowering, but as for these plants foliage is the essential consideration on the showbench, flowers are not vital; but if present they are judged as an asset.

The whole range of ornamental fuchsias is very sensitive to light and to correct cultivation. Their colour varies considerably according to the degree of sunlight received. They tolerate full sunlight and warmer conditions, but if heavily shaded, the colour of the foliage is greatly reduced.

Feeding or the lack of feeding can also produce different results. A fertiliser with a high nitrogen content is preferable to one with high potash. Care must be taken with spraying and watering, as the foliage is easily marked by overhead spraying. The ornamentals prefer a dryish compost, almost to the drying-out stage before the next watering. Leaf-drop can be troublesome if the plants are over-watered, especially in the early stages of growth, and particularly with peat-based composts, as the plants are prone to damp-off at the base. But the most important aspect of their cultivation is the light factor. Judges can only assess what they see on the showbench, and the ornamental or variegated characteristics must be present.

The most attractive and easily obtainable ornamentals include Autumnale (Burning Bush); Cloth of Gold; Golden Marinka; Golden Treasure; and Sunray. The American Fuchsia Society definition of variegated-foliage fuchsias is 'plants that bear leaves having more than one colour. When exhibited the colourfulness of the foliage will be judged rather than floriferousness. Seed berries are permitted'. In Britain the carrying of seed berries would result in down-pointing.

Species Fuchsias

Finding out where the species fuchsia grows in its natural habitat gives clues to how to cultivate it in this country. *F. magellanica* comes from the Magellan area around Tierra del Fuego, the southernmost part of Chile, and is extremely hardy. *F. excorticata*, found in New Zealand, reaches a height of between 30 and 40ft (9 to 12m), whilst *F. procumbens*, with petal-less tubular flowers, is found on the shoreline of New Zealand as a prostrate, creeping plant a few inches high. Some, such as *F. fulgens*, have tuberous roots; others are epiphytic. *F. boliviana (F. corymbiflora)* produces purple berries tasting like a well-seasoned fig, and *F. arborescens* has attractive flowers like a spray of lilac.

Most national and local society schedules include classes for species. Entering these has been made easier recently as the species variants may now be exhibited within the species classes. The most suitable species for the showbench include: *F. arborescens; F. cordifolia; F. denticulata* (often referred to as *F. serratifolia*); *F. fulgens* var *gesneriana; F. procumbens;* and *F. splendens*. They all prefer a loam-based compost and grow better in the traditional clay pot. *F. procumbens*, however, as would be expected, likes a very sandy compost.

Most species resent frequent stopping, and one is usually sufficient. They also differ from other fuchsias in requiring approximately 14 weeks or more from the last stopping to flowering potential. Do not attempt to show as standards, as natural growth is called for in all species classes. Species should be grown on for a few weeks after flowering commences in order to obtain seed pods – not only permitted but desirable. Second-year plants, or even older, are much better for exhibition purposes.

This is a section where correct naming is essential. Keep a special watch on the *Encliandra* section; in the schedule they may be classed as Brevifloras. Not all British Fuchsia Society shows, or most local shows, accept them in the species classes; they have a class set aside for them. Nurseries frequently give incorrect names: a frequent error is listing *F. loxensis* when supplying a hybrid named Speciosa.

F. arborescens will develop a very vigorous root system but needs a lot of restriction to obtain flowering. *F. procumbens* is best shown elevated as a trailer. Some judges down-point this if it is shown without berries; these should not be handled but exhibited with their bloom. *F. fulgens* and its variants make large plants. Four- or five-year plants can have a head of over 4ft (122cm) in an 8in (20cm) or 9in (23cm) pot. This species will take two or three stops but still requires 12 to 14 weeks after the last stop to reach full flower.

Judging Criteria

Species should be grown freely, or with the minimum amount of training that will promote branching. Decorative fruit may be allowed to develop as an added attraction. Clean foliage, fresh flower and/or fruit is expected. Stakes or other training media may be used.

Cultural proficiency: A vigorous flourishing plant growth is wanted, with a quantity of foliage, flowers and/or fruit appropriate to the species concerned. Overall quality must be typical of the species shown. The plant must be in good proportion to its container size. All species should be correctly named. Soil surface should be clean, and free of weed, moss or other debris. The label should be neat, clean and legible.

Triphylla Hybrids and Types

Triphyllas have their own class in the majority of show schedules. The exhibiting of plants not directly derived from the original species *F. triphylla* is now allowed, so triphylla types, such as Billy Green, Leverkusen and Trumpeter, can be included.

The hybrids are frost-shy, needing the protection of glass for overwintering, with a minimum temperature of 40°F (4.4°C). Their foliage is attractive, usually dark green with coloured veins. The flowers have the characteristic long tube and small corolla and petals and are borne in terminal clusters. Growth is upright and bushy, except in Mantilla and Trumpeter, and flowering heavy. For exhibition purposes they prefer a loam-based compost, and flower better in the old conventional clay pot. They resent frequent stopping and excellent specimens can be obtained with only one. They do, however, require a longer period of growth after stopping than other cultivars, 14 weeks being generally acceptable.

Most triphyllas, especially the species *F. triphylla*, tend to shed their lower leaves at the slightest provocation. Unless conditions are ideal, with warmth and humidity, flowers are also inclined to drop prematurely. They will, though, tolerate more direct sunlight than other cultivars. The most suitable for the showbench are: Thalia; Gartenmeister Bonstedt; Mary; and Koralle – all true triphylla hybrids. Billy Green and Leverkusen are outstanding triphylla types, with Billy Green being predominant and excelling on the bench.

Judging Criteria
Exactly as laid down for the bush or shrub.

7 Cultivars for Exhibition

The fuchsia flower is classified into three categories for showing: *single* – flowers with four petals only are classed as single; *semi-double* – these are flowers having five, six or seven petals; *double* – double blooms are those having many layers of petals, and those carrying eight petals or more. Some cultivars throw 'petaloids'. Whereas the petal is a division of the corolla, petaloids are described as small petal-like divisions emerging from the base of the corolla. Sometimes even the stamens have assumed the part of petals.

The various lists of cultivars given here cannot be 'complete', but they should help you select cultivars for exhibiting in different classes and categories. Those marked with an asterisk are considered outstanding.

Baskets (Half)
Autumnale; Blush Dawn; Coachman; Falling Stars; Jack Shahan; *La Campanella; Mrs W. Rundle; Pink Marshmallow; President Stanley Wilson; *Princessita; *Swingtime; Walsingham.

Baskets (Full)
Crackerjack; Daisy Bell; Dusky Rose; Fiery Spider; Golden Marinka; Harry Gray; Jack Acland; Jack Shahan; Kathy Louise; *La Campanella; Lakeside; Lena; *Marinka; Pink Galore; President Stanley Wilson; Princessita; Sophisticated Lady; Swingtime; Trail Blazer.

Bushes and Shrubs
Annabel; Ann H. Tripp; Beacon; Billy Green; Bon Accorde; *Border Queen; *Cambridge Louie; Celia Smedley; *Cloverdale Pearl; Countess of Aberdeen; Dusky Beauty; Flirtation Waltz; Heidi Ann; Lady Isobel Barnett; Lena Dalton; Lindisfarne; Margaret Roe; Mieke Meursing; Mr A. Huggett; Nellie Nuttall; Pacquesa; Pink Darling; Plenty; Royal Velvet; Snowcap; Tom Thumb; *White Joy; Westminster Chimes.

3½in (9cm) Pot Classes
Alwin; *Border Queen; Estelle Marie; *Heidi Ann; *Lena Dalton; Margaret Roe; Micky Goult; Mieke Meursing; Nellie Nuttall; Sandboy; Westminster Chimes.

Espaliers
Border Queen; Coachman; Display; Herald; Jack Acland; Jack Shahan;
Kathy Louise; *Lena; Miss California; *Muriel; Mrs Marshall; President
Stanley Wilson; Swingtime; White Spider.

Floriferous
Border Queen; Cambridge Louie; Lady Isobel Barnett; Mieke Meursing;
Plenty; Westminster Chimes.

Hanging Pots
*Barry's Queen; Border Queen; Cambridge Louie; Cascade; Daisy Bell;
Derby Imp; Harry Gray; Iris Amer; Jack Shahan; *La Campanella; Lena;
Marinka; Princessita; Walsingham; *Westminster Chimes.

Pillars
Barbara; Constance; Herald; *Fascination; Joan Smith; Jack Shahan;
Mephisto; Muriel; Pink Pearl; Rufus; *Snowcap; Swingtime.

Ornamental and Variegated
*Autumnale; *Cloth of Gold; Golden Marinka; Genii; Green-n-Gold; Tom
West.

Pastel-shaded
Blush-o'-Dawn; Cliff's Own; Cliff's Unique; Shady Blue; Shy Lady;
Walsingham.

Pyramids
*Achievement; Amy Lye; Brutus; Celia Smedley; Clipper; Display; Joan
Smith; *Lena; Lye's Unique; Mrs Marshall; Mrs Lovell Swisher; Pink
Darling; *Snowcap.

Red and Whites
Icecap; Nellie Nuttall; Pacquesa; Snowcap; Swingtime.

Species
F. arborescens; F. cordifolia; F. boliviana (F. corymbiflora); F. denticulata; F.
fulgens; *F. fulgens var gesneriana; *F. fulgens var rubra grandiflora; F.
microphylla; *F. procumbens; F. splendens.

Standards (Quarter and Half)
*Bon Accorde; Brilliant; Chang; China Lantern; Countess of Aberdeen;
Dusky Beauty; Lady Thumb; Lindisfarne; Lye's Unique; Margaret Roe;
Micky Goult; Pee Wee Rose; Son of Thumb; *Tom Thumb; White Joy.

Standards (Full)
Achievement; *Barbara; Celia Smedley; Cloverdale Pearl; Display; Dollar Princess; Flirtation Waltz; Hidecote Beauty; *Lady Isobel Barnett; Lye's cultivars (any); Mieke Meursing; Mrs Lovell Swisher; Nancy Lou; Other Fellow; Pink Darling; Shady Blue; Snowcap.

Standards (Miniature)
Bobby Wingrove; Christmas Elf; Cloverdale Jewel; Countess of Aberdeen; Curly Q; Derby Imp; Dusky Beauty; Joan's Delight; Little Beauty; *Minirose; Northway; Papoose; Ravensbarrow; Son of Thumb; Tom Woods; Tsjiep; *Westminster Chimes.

Standards (Weeping)
Auntie Jinks; Bouffant; Daisy Bell; Dusky Rose; Fiery Spider; Hula Girl; Jack Acland; *La Campanella; Lena; Marinka; *Mrs W. Rundle; Pink Galore; *Pink Marshmallow; White Spider.

Triphylla (and Types)
*Billy Green; Gartenmeister Bonstedt; Koralle; Leverkusen; Mary; *Thalia.

Whites
Ann H. Tripp; Annabel; Bobby Shaftoe; *Countess of Aberdeen; Flying Cloud; Frank Unsworth; Harry Gray; Roy Walker; Ting-a-Ling; *White Joy.

Cultivars with British Fuchsia Society Awards

First Class Certificate
Annabel; Billy Green; Border Queen; Celia Smedley; Display; Joy Patmore; Marinka; Royal Velvet; Snowcap; Swingtime.

Award of Merit
Citation; Cloverdale Pearl; Eva Boerg; Genii; Heidi Ann; La Campanella; Mieke Meursing; Mrs Popple; Nellie Nuttall; Pacquesa; Tennessee Waltz; Thalia; Tom Thumb.

Highly Commended
Alison Ewart; Checkerboard; Citation; Flirtation Waltz; Lady Isobel Barnett; Leonora; Margaret Roe; Marin Glow; Tennessee Waltz.

8 The Show

Accredited judges work in accordance with standards approved by the British Fuchsia Society, at national and local level, to achieve a uniform standard in judging. As one of many years' standing, I know we are always looking for growth which is vigorous, uniform, clean and with an abundance of bloom. But the first task judges perform is the checking of pot sizes, and the length of clear stem in classes for standards. They check for double blooms in single classes and vice-versa, and make sure plants are exhibited in the pots in which grown, with special emphasis upon the 3½in (9cm) classes. Any plants grown on the ring culture or double-potted methods will not escape their attention.

This emphasises how carefully would-be winners must study the show schedule beforehand, particularly the definitions, such as the size and type of pot permitted. Showmen have run into trouble with some plastic pots, which until recently were manufactured to almost the same depth (or height) as the diameter. Pots today, especially the continental types, are shallower, and some are deeper. The British Fuchsia Society has altered its definition of standard pots to read: 'The inside diameter at the top should be approximate to the perpendicular height. Half pots are not permitted.' As local shows are usually judged in accordance with BFS standards, these remarks are also applicable there. Square pots or 'Long Toms' would receive a NAS (Not as Schedule), as would pots larger than the size specified in the schedule. The definition applied here is: 'The diameter of a pot is the inside diameter as near to the top as possible, but without including any part of the roll of the rim.' Be careful when using old clay pots, especially those excellent hand-thrown pots; all can measure more than the intended size. An intended 6in (15cm) pot very often finishes up measuring 6½in (16.5cm).

Most classes in the schedule indicate the size of pot permitted. 'In a pot not exceeding 6½in (16.5cm)' does not mean that a plant cannot be exhibited in a pot smaller than the maximum specified. Where the schedule calls for 'Three plants of any cultivar or cultivars in 4in (10cm), 5in (12.5cm), 6in (15cm)' no latitude is allowed on size. Plants must be exhibited in the sizes indicated; the wording does not mean 'not exceeding'. When exhibiting in a class specifying 'in any size pot' make sure you still use a standard pot, not a shrub pot or a container with straight sides.

Never enter a species fuchsia in any class quoting 'any cultivar or variety'; it will be NAS. You could enter a species in a class calling for 'A fuchsia plant, single' or for 'A basket of fuchsias only'. If the schedule calls for 'one plant of a species' do not exhibit one of the species variants. It will be considered NAS by many judges, and cannot be shown as a cultivar either. Pay particular attention to the *Encliandra* section; many shows have classes for these, generally under the name of Brevifloras. BFS shows, and those judged under their standards, will not accept them in the species classes.

When entering multi-pot classes, especially classes for two plants judged as a pair, the prime consideration is balance. Every plant should be matched and approximately the same size and shape. Should the class call for different or distinct cultivars, enter just that – nothing causes more heartaches to judges than having to 'NAS' superb entries for the very common fault of including more than one cultivar of a particular variety. Border Queen and Eden Lady, two sister seedlings, although distinct and separate cultivars are so similar it is wise not to enter the two together in classes requiring distinct cultivars. In the 'hardy' classes, enter only cultivars included in the hardy list issued by the BFS; if not on the list your cultivar will not be eligible, whether the plant is actually hardy or not. (These lists are revised from time to time.)

For the variegated or ornamental foliage classes, make sure your plant's foliage has not reverted to plain green; the judge will assess what is in front of him, so the variegation or ornamental effect must be present. A typical offending cultivar is Genii when given too much shading.

Judges take into consideration the degree of skill offered by the exhibitor. Some cultivars, such as Blush-o'-Dawn, Citation or Gruss aus dem Bodethal (synonymous with Black Prince) are notoriously difficult to train for the showbench. Barbara is extremely easy to train as a standard, but a different proposition to shape as a bush or shrub. Such points do not go unheeded.

Plants must be floriferous, typically so for the cultivar concerned. Snowcap and Lady Isobel Barnett, for instance, together with Mieke Meursing, have to be smothered in flower for even initial recognition from the judges. Judges no longer 'NAS' plants bearing flowers with more than four petals shown in classes for singles; such plants are now down-pointed. Do not be tempted to show the same plant in classes for doubles; its fate would probably be the same, this time because the majority of its flowers are not double. Such plants should be eliminated from your show selection. A few cultivars which cannot make up their minds whether they are single or double include Tom Thumb; Estelle Marie; Leonora; Pacquesa; Mieke Meursing; Coquet Bell; and Twinkling Stars for throwing more than the permitted four sepals.

One-sided plants, except fans and espaliers, are overlooked at once; yellowing, bruised or damaged foliage, or leaves infected with pests, all lose points, or even disqualify the plant. Spent seed-pods and faded blooms are the commonest faults, again losing valuable points. Supports and canes are permitted, but they should be unobtrusive.

Although the British Fuchsia Society no longer uses a points system, many judges keep in mind the pointing previously used, which allocated 6 points for cultivation, 6 for quality and quantity of flower, 6 for quality of foliage and 2 for presentation. They pay particular attention to foliage: gross over-feeding can be detected on sight, the excessive content of potash being reflected in the pale colour and leathery condition of the leaves. Again, judges must judge what is in front of them.

Judges do not penalise exhibits which are unnamed, but in close competition that could be the deciding factor. If you are in doubt of the correct name of your cultivar, a little card saying 'Judges please name' will receive their expert attention. Most judges are available after judging to give advice on the exhibits.

When entering as a 'beginner', you must not have won an award of any description at any previous BFS or affiliated society show, but you may enter in any class in the schedule. A 'novice' is one who has not won a first prize except in a beginners' class at any previous BFS or affiliated show, and may enter any class in the schedule, except the beginners'.

Getting Your Fuchsias to the Show

It is all too easy to find that some of your flowers are bruised or laterals broken on arrival at the show. Try the following method. Purchase a roll of butter muslin from a car-accessory store; it is also known as stockinette muslin, from the mill finisher. A roll 15in (38cm) wide, in the form of a sleeve, is enough to protect twenty-odd bush/shrub or standard plants.

After the plant has been dressed and watered, cut approximately 24in (60cm) of sleeving and then roll it on your arm just above your right wrist, ready for opening in the next operation. Hold the rim of the pot in the horizontal position with the same hand. The left hand is opening the sleeving for the next operation. Still in the horizontal position, the sleeving on the left hand is beginning to be placed over the pot. Turn the plant completely upside down with the hands in the same position. The left hand is now gently opening the sleeving and easing it up over the base of the plant. The operation is continued until the whole plant has been covered. The blooms and leaves will hang upside-down naturally in a semi-limp condition, and no harm is caused by the contact of the muslin.

During the entire operation the hands remain exactly the same, each carrying out its own operation. When the covering is completed the whole of the pot is free, but the whole of the plant is covered, in the shape of a large ball with the top left open. Some exhibitors take a slightly longer sleeve and completely cover the top of the plant, inserting a cane centrally and tying the sleeve to the central cane. Personally, I do not like sticking canes into the root ball, as some damage to the root system must occur.

After arriving at the show, hold the plant upside-down, and merely roll the sleeving inside-out, exposing the plant, without a single bloom damaged. Give the plant a shake and with an upward movement reverse its flowers and foliage to their natural position. In this way thirty-odd plants can be packed close together in an average 1300 family saloon car, and will travel hundreds of miles

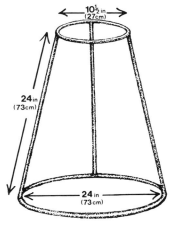

Iron stand for transporting baskets

without trouble. Standards can have their heads dealt with in the same way – and with a little ingenuity so could other structures.

Transporting Baskets
The transportation of baskets, measuring up to 5ft (150cm) across when fully laden with bloom, creates particular problems. I have eventually found an ideal solution – having stands made up by the local blacksmith. Of ⅜in (9.5mm) mild steel, these consist of one bottom ring 24in (60cm) across the base, and a top ring 10½in (26.7cm) wide for the basket to rest upon. Three supporting arms 24in (60cm) long are welded to the rings, holding the stand together (see drawing). The baskets are just lifted from their stands or hooks in the greenhouse, placed on top of the transporting stands and carried out to the van. The stands are also useful for displaying large specimen plants in large pots on the terrace and patio.

Staging your Plants

Judges expect to see plants properly 'dressed': many exhibitors, through lack of time or experience, fail to present their plants at their best. Scores of flowers are left hidden in the foliage – ease them all out with a pen or similar instrument. One cultivar notorious for hiding its flowers is Iced Champagne, and many basket-type cultivars do this too. With the gentle teasing-out of blooms, mediocre-looking plants have been transformed into award-winning exhibits. The popping of blooms prematurely will often result in the plant being down-pointed.

Give yourself plenty of time to stage your exhibits. Turn the plant upside-down, if possible, shaking out yellowing and damaged leaves and spent flowers, letting the entire growth fall back naturally into position; water well. Take along a few spare plants, a spare cane or two and additional pots – especially where classes call for more than one plant. In the multi-pot classes, use colour-blending to effect. Lift either back or front plants if that helps to obtain correct balance.

Finally, always remember the astounding fact that your plants look twice as good on the showbench as on your own staging in the greenhouse.

Fuchsia Societies

Societies are now established in most temperate countries of the world. The main difference between those in Britain and elsewhere is whereas British shows are largely competitive, the emphasis in other countries is placed on exhibiting. The British Fuchsia Society with well over 6,000 members is easily the largest; it was formed in 1938 with the object of furthering interest in the cultivation of the fuchsia.

The membership subscription (£4 per annum for single and £5 for joint membership in 1984) allows free admission to most shows and a copy of the Society's *Handbook of Judging Standards*. Members have the right to exhibit free of charge at any show organised by the Society. They are entitled to the *Fuchsia Annual* and Bulletins, in addition to free advice on matters concerning fuchsia culture. Shows are currently held during the summer in London, Manchester (Sale), Birmingham, Reading, Chippenham, Harrogate and Central Scotland. The Honorary Secretary at the time of writing is R. Ewart, 29 Princess Crescent, Dollar, Clackmannshire.

Local societies, most of which are affiliated to the BFS, are established in all parts of Britain and in Ireland. All hold regular meetings, with talks and lectures, and hold their own individual shows. Details of your nearest society are available from the BFS Secretary or the author.

Index